THE
ALPHABET
IN NATURE

THE
ALPHABET

Sunset with its reflection in Lake Michigan
© Jerry Hennen

IN NATURE

BY JUDY FELDMAN

ᑭ CHILDRENS PRESS ®

CHICAGO

The cover image is a West Indian flamingo from the Caribbean.
© Gerry Ellis/Ellis Wildlife Collection

Series cover and interior design by Sara Shelton

Library of Congress Cataloging-in-Publication Data

Feldman, Judy.
  The alphabet in nature/Judy Feldman.
     p.   cm.—(Wordless concept books)
  Summary: Explores the alphabet through photographs of animals and nature scenes.
  ISBN 0-516-05101-6
  1. Nature—Pictorial works—Juvenile literature.   2. English
language—Alphabet—Juvenile literature. [1. Animals.   2. Nature.   3. Alphabet.]
I. Title.   II. Series.
QH46.F34 1991
(E)—dc20   90-22315
                                                                            CIP
                                                                            AC

ABCDEF

GHIJKL

MNOPQ

RSTUV

WXYZ

A

Dewdrops on grass
© Pam Hickman/Valan

B

A snake
© Jerry Hennen

C

The head of a bighorn ram
© Anthony Mercieca/Root Resources

D

A damselfly laying eggs
© Jerry Hennen

E

Detail of brain coral from Andros Island, Bahamas
© Jeff Rotman

F

A blue-throated hummingbird in flight
© Wayne Lankinen/Valan

G

Grass seen magnified under a microscope
© Harold V. Green/Valan

H

Thick white crystals of frost on grass stems
© Stephen J. Krasemann/Valan

I

A ground squirrel from Door County, Wisconsin
© Jerry Hennen

J

A Monarch caterpillar changing to a chrysalis
© Jerry Hennen

K

A black-bellied plover in winter
© Francis Lepine/Valan

L

A black-and-green bush viper from Africa
© Mary Clay/Tom Stack & Associates

M

A Dall ram in early winter
© Johnny Johnson/Valan

N

A maple tree trunk
© Ian Davis-Young/Valan

The cross section of a Douglas fir tree
© J.R. Page/Valan

P

The fiddlehead of an ostrich fern
© Harold V. Green/Valan

Q

A beaver grooming itself
© Wayne Lankinen/Valan

R

Saguaro cacti from the southwest
© Jerry Hennen

S

A West Indian flamingo from the Caribbean
© Gerry Ellis/Ellis Wildlife Collection

T

A mushroom growing wild
© MacDonald/Photri

U

The face of a waterbuck
© Stan Osolinski/Root Resources

V

The head of a Blacktail jackrabbit
© Stan Osolinski/Root Resources

A rock formation in Monument Valley, Arizona
© Gerry Ellis/Ellis Wildlife Collection

X

A spider on a web in Barbados
© Dr. A. Farquhar/Valan

Y

The tail of a diving humpback whale
© R. Galbraith/Valan

Z

The head and long neck of a Western grebe
© Wayne Lankinen/Valan

This book has no words. It doesn't need any. The idea is for you, parents and children together, to supply the words while sharing a fun new way of looking at nature and learning about letters.

Judy Feldman